A First Look at Art

Myths

RUTH THOMSON

Chrysalis Children's Books

First published in the UK in 2005 by
Chrysalis Children's Books,
An imprint of Chrysalis Books Group Plc,
The Chrysalis Building, Bramley Road,
London W10 6SP

ISBN 1 84458 199 3

British Library Cataloguing in Publication Data for this book
is available from the British Library.

Editorial manager *Joyce Bentley*
Project manager *Rasha Elsaeed*
Editor *Susie Brooks*
Designers *Rachel Hamdi, Holly Mann*
Picture researcher *Claire Gouldstone*
Photographer *Jerry Moeran*
Consultant *Erika Langmuir, formerly Head of Education,
The National Gallery, London, UK*

The author and publishers would like to thank Susan Keverne
and pupils at King Alfred School, Hampstead, London; Liz
Burton, Eleanor Howard, Clare Whyles, Jill Pennington and
pupils at St Ebbe's School, Oxford; and Claudia Celder, for
their contributions to this book.

Printed in China

Typography *Natascha Frensch*
Read Regular, READ SMALLCAPS and Read Space; European
Community Design Registration 2003 and Copyright ©
Natascha Frensch 2001-2004 Read Medium, **Read Black**
and *Read Slanted* Copyright © Natascha Frensch 2003-2004

READ™ is a revolutionary new typeface that will enchance
children's understanding through clear, easily recognisable
character shapes. With its evenly spaced and carefully
designed characters, READ™ will help children at all stages
to improve their literacy skills and is ideal for young readers,
reluctant readers and especially children with dyslexia.

Contents

MAGICAL MYTHS

Myths are ancient stories that tell mainly of gods, superhuman heroes and strange or magical creatures. Some myths explain local beliefs. Others account for natural wonders, such as lightning and earthquakes, that people long ago did not understand. Artists throughout history have recorded myths from all around the world.

In this book you will find images of imaginary creatures, heroic characters and scenes from mythical stories. You will discover what inspired the artists and learn about their techniques. There are also questions to help you look at each work in detail, and ideas for creating your own mythical pictures and models.

◉ *You'll find answers to the questions and information about the artists on pages 30-31.*

Hydria (water jar)
Maker unknown
c650 BC, (43 cm high)

Picture hunt
✧ Picture hunt boxes suggest other artists and artworks that you might like to look at.

Arty tips
✧ Look out for Arty tips boxes that suggest handy techniques and materials to use in your own work.

Decorative jars

In ancient Greece, artists painted mythical scenes on jars. They designed the pictures to fit the curved shape. The jar on the left shows the last part of the story of heroic Hercules.

Hercules was set 12 fearsome tasks by his cousin King Eurystheus. His final challenge was to capture Cerberus, the fierce three-headed dog that guarded the land of the dead. In this scene we see Hercules leading the beast to the king, who has jumped into a pot in fear!

Notice how the style of painting is very flat and simple. The artist has used a different colour for each of the dog's heads, giving a feeling of movement.

Caught on canvas

Even in more recent times, the drama of Greek myths has inspired artists. The painting above shows the ancient Greek character Prometheus bringing fire to Earth, having stolen it from the gods. His billowing orange robes echo the leaping, glowing flames as he looks back slyly at the heavens. But the dark clouds hint at the punishment he will soon receive for what he has done.

Prometheus
Stealing Fire
Jan Cossiers
1637 (182
x 113 cm)

WHAT A HERO!

Perseus was a Greek mythic hero, famed for killing the snake-headed monster Medusa. Here, we see him saving the princess Andromeda, who is being sacrificed to an evil sea beast.

The sacrifice was a punishment from Neptune, king of the sea. He was furious because Andromeda's mother had boasted that her daughter was prettier than any sea nymph.

Perseus Rescuing Andromeda
Piero di Cosimo
c1515 (71 x 123 cm)

◉ *Can you spot the three pictures of Perseus?*

Frightening focus

Our eye is drawn to the sea monster in the centre, lurching fiercely towards the princess, who is tied to a rock. Blood spurts out where Perseus slashes the monster's neck. The water churns as the monster tries to push Perseus off his back.

◉ *What is Andromeda trying to do?*
◉ *How can you tell this is a sea monster, rather than a land monster?*

Storytellers

The figures on the left express their grief at Andromeda's capture. The people on the right rejoice at her release.

◉ *How do their poses differ?*

Heroic action

There are three images of Perseus in this painting. He flies in wearing magic, winged sandals, slays the monster, then celebrates with the people. The action moves back and forth across the picture.

CRAZY CHARACTERS

Scary sea monsters

Paint your own picture of a scary, imaginary sea monster.

◉ Draw a sketch first, showing all the monster's horrible features – perhaps it has sharp teeth, spikes, horns or tusks. Decide what shape it will be – long, short, thin or fat.

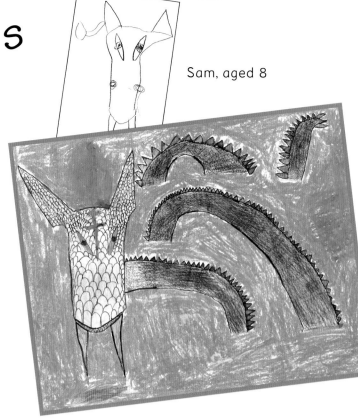

Sam, aged 8

◉ If your monster is swimming at the surface, show only some parts of its body above the water.

◉ Paint your monster, or make a collage, using dramatic colours.

Anya, aged 9

Robin and Jack, both aged 8

Arty tips

✰ To make your sea monster look very fierce, make its eyes, teeth or tongue extra big.

✰ Use curving shapes to create a sense of movement.

Here-and-now heroes

What would a modern flying hero look like? What might he or she do? Create a collage showing your ideas.

Cas, aged 6

◉ Draw a striking city scene or landscape for the background.
◉ Make a collage hero and glue him or her in place.

Jack, aged 6

Picture hunt

✫ Compare other pictures of Perseus, such as **Perseus on Pegasus Hastening to the Rescue of Andromeda** by Lord Frederic Leighton and **Perseus and Andromeda** by Joachim Wtewael.

Computer creations

Use a computer drawing program to design a monster or a hero.
◉ Use bold colours and shapes.
◉ Why not invent a wacky name for your creation?

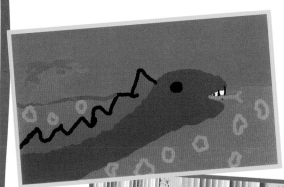

Emily, aged 8

Andrew, aged 8

Phoenix, aged 8

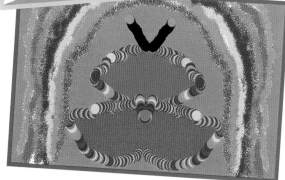

Shannon and Leah, aged 7

A BRILLIANT BATTLE

The ancient Indian poem Ramayana tells the story of Prince Rama, whose wife Sita was kidnapped by Ravana the demon king. More than 400 images bring the poem to life. This one shows Rama's last battle with Ravana. Rama is the warrior with blue face and hands.

Rama's army includes his brother and Hanuman the monkey god. They fire arrows at Ravana but fail to kill him. Rama tries to cut off the king's ten heads, but they keep growing back.

◉ *How many heads can you spot?*
◉ *Why has the artist shown so many?*

Ramayana, Yuddha
Kanda, *Sahib Din*
1652 (21 x 35 cm)

Final victory

Then Rama fires an arrow with divine powers that pierces Ravana's heart. Rama thanks his friends for their help.

◉ *Follow the story in pictures. How many times does Rama appear?*

◉ *What is he doing in each image?*

Bright patterns

The picture was painted in brilliant colours on handmade paper. There are no shadows. Heroes, demons and animals have clear outlines. Notice that all the faces are drawn in profile (seen from the side).

RAMA-DRAMA
Picture a story

Read the story of the Ramayana. Use the crisp style of the Indian painters to illustrate one of the exciting events.

◉ Draw your picture in outline first.

◉ Colour it in, being very careful not to go over the outlines. Use bright, vivid colours.

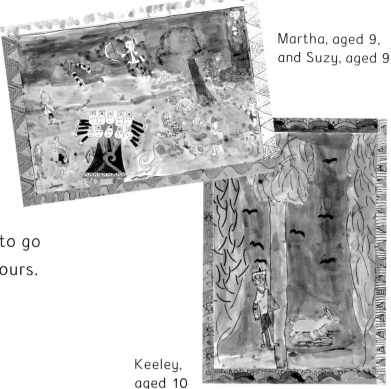

Martha, aged 9, and Suzy, aged 9

Keeley, aged 10

Jonny, aged 9

◉ You could illustrate the whole story as a group project. Each person should illustrate a different key event. Then arrange the pictures in sequence, to tell the whole story.

Ben, aged 10

Clara, aged 9

Alec and Phoenix, Nikhil and Jake, all aged 9

Cut-out King

Make a huge cut-out of Ravana.

◉ Cut out ten separate heads from card. Make a gold crown for each one and glue them in place.

◉ Draw on Ravana's faces. Use wool for eyebrows, hair and moustaches.

◉ Cut out a card body and legs and decorate them however you like.

◉ Make arms from card and create a different weapon for each hand to hold.

◉ Glue all of Ravana's parts together and then stick him to a stack of joined boxes, so that he stands up.

A group of Year 4 children

Fahema, aged 9, and
Zahra, aged 10

Setting the scene

Make a colourful paper collage of Ravana preparing for battle.

◉ First sketch out the scene.

◉ Glue down torn paper pieces, following the lines of your sketch.

◉ Use shiny paper to emphasise Ravana's crowns and costume.

Arty tip

✫ Scrumple small pieces of tissue into balls to make textured flowers, trees and clouds.

Alfred, aged 9, and Rina, aged 10

TRANSFORMATIONS

These two pictures show characters from Greek mythology who are both turned into plants.
We see them at different stages of transformation.

Apollo and Daphne, *Antonio del Pollaiuolo*
c1470–1480
(29.5 x 20 cm)

Branching out

In Pollaiuolo's picture, the beautiful nymph Daphne is turning into a bay tree in the arms of the god Apollo.

Cupid, the god of love, wanted revenge because Apollo had teased him. So he made Apollo fall in love with Daphne, but ensured that she would never love him back.

Daphne called to her father, a river god, to stop Apollo pursuing her. In a flash, her toes took root, her chest grew bark and her arms became leafy branches.

◉ *Why do you think the artist has focused on Daphne's changing arms?*
◉ *From their expressions, how do you think Daphne and Apollo are feeling?*
◉ *What tells you that Apollo has been running?*
◉ *Why did the artist include a river?*

A flowery fate

Narcissus was a beautiful youth, who was made to fall hopelessly in love with his own reflection. He pined away until all that was left of him was a flower that grew in watery places and bent at the neck.

This picture of him is a huge tapestry, woven from coloured wool. It was designed for the wall of a grand house.

◉ *Why is Narcissus surrounded by a carpet of flowers?*

◉ *What animals and birds can you see?*

Narcissus, *Unknown French, or Franco-Flemish, tapestry maker, c1490-1510 (282 x 311 cm)*

GROWING WILD

Tree trickery

Draw your own picture of Daphne turning into a tree.

◉ You could do a sequence of drawings to show how different parts of her gradually transform into parts of a tree.

◉ Or you may prefer to draw a single picture that shows her part human and part tree.

Robyn, aged 7

Susie, aged 9, and Zoë, aged 10

Animal magic

Imagine someone turning into an animal instead.

◉ Create a picture that gives clues to show what the animal is, but also includes parts of a person.

Jenny and Clara, both aged 9

Poppy, aged 9

Arty tip

☆ Think carefully how to show that a tree or an animal was once a person.

• Will you show a human face or hands?

• Will you change the hair, body or feet?

• What colour will you paint the body?

Flowers forever

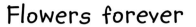

Create a flowery design
for a tapestry.

◉ Draw your design in wax crayon
or oil pastels, using only three or
four colours.

Asim, aged 6

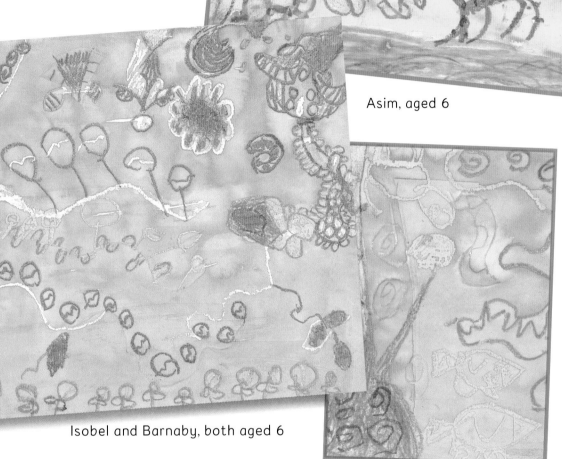

Isobel and Barnaby, both aged 6

◉ Brush watery paint or ink over the paper.
Your design will show through.

Sammy, aged 6

Jake, aged 6

Picture hunt

✬ Look at two series of tapestries
called **The Hunt of the Unicorn** and
Lady and the Unicorn. These depict
the mythical unicorn (a white pony
with a goat's beard and a single
horn). They were made at around
the same time as **Narcissus** and
are also full of images of plants
and animals.

Salmon People, *Unknown Tlingit artist, collected in 1898 (44.5 cm high)*

Artists have often been inspired by mythical creatures that are half human and either half fish, half bird or half mammal.

The Salmon People

The Pacific Northwest Coast Indians treated salmon with great respect. They believed them to be people in another form, who lived in a village under the sea. The painted wooden sculptures on the left show the fishy-human nature of the Salmon People.

Strange sculptures

The far left-hand sculpture shows half a fish and half a man. Notice the fish gills on the man's body and how his hand doubles as the fish's fin.

The second sculpture shows a human *inside* a whole fish. He has both an arm and a fin. The fishy tail is split and doubles as the man's legs.

◉ *What similarities do you notice between the two sculptures?*

◉ *What parts of the fish echo their human forms?*

Musical mermaids

Mermaids are mythical creatures with the head and torso of a beautiful woman and the tail of a fish. They were said to sing so sweetly that they charmed sailors to follow them to the bottom of the sea. This painted terracotta mermaid plays a guitar to accompany her singing.

◉ *What can you see attached to her? Why might the artist have included these particular things?*

Mermaid
Josefina Aguilar
1989
(15 cm high)

CURIOUS CREATURES

Marvellous mermaids

Make a glittery model of a mermaid.

◉ Make the rough shape of the mermaid. Tape together an empty water bottle and a cardboard roll for the body, crumpled newspaper for the head and rolled newspaper for the arms. Cut a card tail.

Cissy, aged 11

◉ Cover the mermaid with several layers of newspaper, and then white tissue paper, dipped in PVA glue. Leave it to dry.

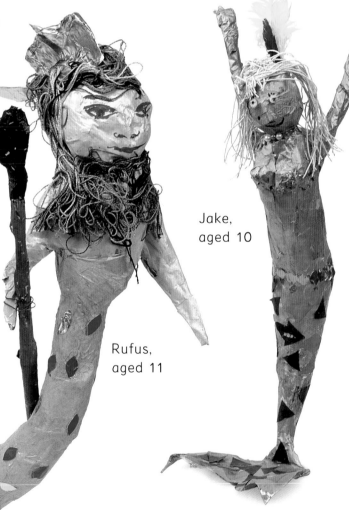

Alice, aged 10

Cara, aged 11

Jake, aged 10

Rufus, aged 11

Arty tips

☆ Use coloured embroidery thread, wool, raffia or string for hair.

☆ Use gummed paper squares, glitter, beads, sequins, shiny paper and gold paint for the decoration.

◉ Paint the mermaid all over, either in one or several colours. Leave it to dry before you paint the face and decorate the body.

Mixed-up models

Make a mythical creature – either one that is half human and half animal, or one that is a mixture of several animals.

◉ Use the papier mâché technique described on the left-hand page.

A SEA MONSTER
Spike, aged 11

A HARPY

Alex, aged 10

◉ Decorate your creature, bringing out its special qualities such as large wings, a whipping tail, wild hair or a terrifying face.

PEGASUS
Kate, aged 10

Picture hunt

✧ Look for other images of creatures that are half human and half animal, such as a **sphinx** (half lion), a **centaur** (half horse), a **harpy** (half bird) or the **Minotaur** (half bull).

✧ Find pictures of creatures made up from different animals, such as **Pegasus** (a horse with wings), the **griffon** (an eagle's head and wings on a lion's body) and the **basilisk** (a rooster-like monster with a snake's tail).

FLYING AND FALLING

In Greek mythology, the great inventor Daedulus was once imprisoned on an island with his son Icarus. To help them both escape, he made two sets of feathery wings, held together with wax.

The wings worked, but the foolish Icarus flew too close to the sun. The wax in his wings melted in the heat, and he plummeted into the sea and drowned.

Up in the sky

Matisse's paper cut-out shows Icarus silhouetted against a starry sky. The figure, with its clumsy short legs and long body, fills the whole height of the picture. The tilt of his arms and head suggest movement.

◉ *Does Icarus look as if he is soaring or falling?*

◉ *What is the red spot on Icarus' body? Why do you think Matisse included this?*

◉ *From his pose, how do you think Icarus is feeling?*

Icarus, *Henri Matisse, 1945 (40.5 x 27 cm)*

Down to earth

Chagall has painted Icarus falling – not towards the sea, but towards a crowded village. The blurry areas, swaying figures and swirly brushstrokes all create a sense of dizzy movement. Spiky marks on the sun suggest its fierce and dangerous heat.

The Fall of Icarus, *Marc Chagall, 1975 (213 x 198 cm)*

The image is full of expression. We feel scared and sorry for Icarus as he falls through the sky.

◉ *How has Chagall used colours to help tell the story?*

◉ *How are the onlookers reacting?*

FEATHERED FIGURES

Up to the sun

Paint a picture of Icarus flying.

◉ Use watery paint to cover a sheet of paper in the colours of a glowing sky. You could include the sea below, too.

Lucas, aged 10

◉ Cut a circle of thin card for the sun.

◉ Cover it with torn strips of red, orange, pink and gold paper. These colours will help create a feeling of heat.

◉ From black card, cut out a winged Icarus.

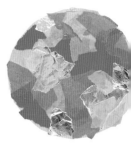

Lucas, aged 10

Ali, aged 9

May, aged 10

Coral, aged 11

Picture hunt

✫ Compare how other artists have depicted the story of Icarus, such as **Landscape with Fall of Icarus** by Pieter Breughel the Elder; **The Lament for Icarus** by Herbert Draper and **Fall of Icarus** by Carlo Saraceni. Which do you prefer and why?

◉ *Before you stick the sun and Icarus on to the background, arrange them in several ways to see which effect you like best.*

• *Does the sun look better in the middle or to one side?*

• *Does Icarus look more dramatic near the sun or falling down towards the sea?*

Ready to fly

Make a papier mâché model
of Icarus and his feathered wings.

◉ Follow the steps on page 20 for
making a papier mâché figure.

◉ Make a separate set of wings by
sticking coloured feathers on to card.

◉ When your model is dry, glue the
wings in place.

Joe, aged 10

Birdman

Alternatively, make a model of a birdman. Give
it a bird's head, beak and feathery wings, but a
human's body, arms and legs.

Stephan,
aged 11

Esther,
aged 10

Arty tips

✧ Add sparkly sequins, shiny paper or glitter
to Icarus' costume to make him glint in the light

✧ If you can't find any feathers for the wings,
use wisps of cotton wool instead. Try dying
them with coloured ink or food colouring.

DECORATIVE DRAGONS

According to Chinese mythology, dragons were wise, friendly and kind. People believed that in winter dragons buried themselves at the bottom of the sea. In spring, they flew into the sky to live among the clouds and brought rain, the key to life. They had magical powers and could change shape, size and colour.

Majestic beast

The dragon was a symbol for the Chinese ruler – the emperor – and his family. Notice the dragon decorations on this embroidered imperial robe.

Earth and heaven

The other decorations illustrate the Chinese idea of Earth and heaven. The coloured stripes at the bottom symbolise the elements of nature – earth, fire, water, metal and wood. The mountains and the waves represent land and sea. Around them are all sorts of other symbols linked with power, wisdom and good luck.

Dragon Robe for a Woman
of the Imperial Family
1880-1911, Qing Dynasty
(144.7 x 199.5 cm)

Spot the symbols

◉ *Can you find these symbols on the robe?*

 The **five-toed dragon** symbolises the emperor's power to move between heaven and Earth – just as dragons do – and to ensure his people's well-being.

 Mountains are symbols of the Earth, and also of strength and stability.

 The **constellation of three stars** is a symbol of the Universe.

 The **pair of bronze cups** symbolise respect for one's parents. One shows a tiger (strength) and the other a monkey (intelligence).

 The **water weed** is a symbol of purity.

 Fire represents brilliant thought.

 The **axe** symbolises the power of the emperor to punish others.

 The **red bat** is a symbol of happiness – in Chinese, the words for bat and for happiness sound the same.

 This **Chinese symbol** for double happiness indicates a wedding.

 The **pearl** held by the central dragon is a symbol of wisdom.

CHINESE CHUMS

Dazzling dragons

Look carefully at pictures of Chinese dragons and make sketches of their shapes and features.

◉ Make a large collage of a dragon, using your sketch as inspiration.

◉ Cut out a card head and body.

◉ Glue on pieces of felt, tissue paper, shiny paper, cotton wool or sequins for the face, scales and claws.

Oscar, aged 10

Caitlan, aged

Matthew F, aged 10

Makena, aged 10

Olivia, aged 10

Caitlan, aged 10

Picture hunt

✦ Look out for Chinese sculptures of dragons, and painted images on Chinese porcelain dishes, vases and plates.

✦ Compare Chinese dragons with Western images of dragons. Look at pictures of **Saint George and the Dragon** by Paolo Uccello, Jacopo Tintoretto, Raphael, Gustave Moreau, Bernardo Martorell and others.

Dazzling dragons

The dragon is one of the animals of the Chinese zodiac. Look for the year you were born on the zodiac chart below to find out which animal you are.

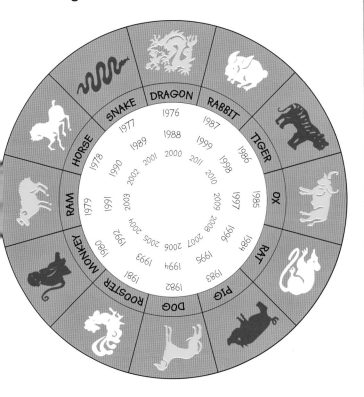

Animal characters

A person born in the year of a particular animal is said to be similar in character to that animal. Is this true for you?

Rat cool, charming and a perfectionist

Ox loyal, quiet, patient, hot-tempered and alert

Tiger brave, indecisive and sympathetic

Rabbit dreamy, kind, ambitious and lucky

Dragon honest, energetic, brave and healthy

Snake wise, helpful and softly-spoken

Horse popular, cheerful and independent

Ram gentle, shy, elegant and intelligent

Monkey clever, flexible and skilful

Rooster hard-working, capable and lucky

Dog loyal, responsible, good at keeping secrets

Pig determined, brave and a good friend

◉ Make a colourful round picture of your zodiac animal to put on your bedroom door or wall.

THE YEAR OF THE ROOSTER
1993

Olivia, aged 10

Alexia,
aged 10

Julian,
aged 10

THE YEAR OF THE DOG
1994

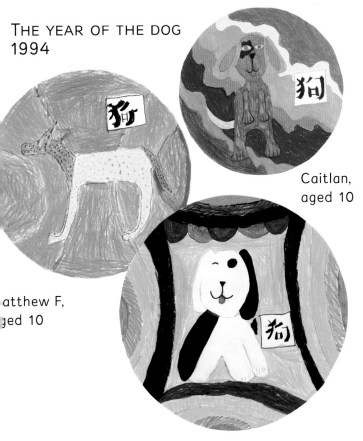

Caitlan,
aged 10

atthew F,
ged 10

Nina, aged 10

ARTISTS AND ANSWERS

MAGICAL MYTHS (pages 4/5)

ABOUT JAN COSSIERS

Cossiers (1600-1671) lived in Antwerp (now in Belgium). He studied as a portrait painter and travelled throughout Italy and France. His early works were life-sized scenes of gypsies and fortune tellers. Later, he worked with the artist Peter Paul Rubens, making paintings of his designs. He then went on to create Biblical scenes for churches.

ABOUT ANCIENT GREEK JARS

Greek pottery jars and vases were first decorated with this black-figure technique in Athens during the seventh century BC. Artists painted black silhouettes with engraved lines for the details, and added red and white elements

WHAT A HERO!
(pages 6/7)

Answers for page 7

• Andromeda is struggling to escape from her ties.
• The monster has webbed feet and tusks like a walrus, suggesting it is a sea monster.
• The grieving people cower and cover their eyes. Those celebrating raise their arms and look upward.

ABOUT PIERO DI COSIMO

Piero (c1461/62-1522) came from Florence, Italy. He took his name from the artist Cosimo Rosselli, who taught him to paint. Piero assisted Rosselli with the decoration of the walls of the Sistine Chapel in Rome. He painted church altarpieces, murals and portraits as well as mythologies. He also worked on designs for festivals and processions. He made his mythological beasts and invented creatures seem real, by putting together parts of animals that people already knew.

A BRILLIANT BATTLE (pages 10/11)

Answers for page 11

• There are 20 cut-off heads of Ravana. This is twice as many as he had, to show that they kept growing back.

• There are three images of Rama. In the first, he fires arrows from his chariot. In the second, he blesses his brother, Lakshamana, in thanks for his help. In the third, he hugs Hanuman the monkey god, applauded by monkeys from Hanuman's army

ABOUT SAHIB DIN

Sahib Din (active 1628-1653) was an Indian artist. He was probably the master of a workshop that produced court paintings and illustrated manuscripts for the king of the city of Udaipur. A team of illustrators worked on a whole manuscript and two artists worked on each picture. The master painted the outlines and key details, such as faces. The less experienced artists filled in the colours.

TRANSFORMATIONS (pages 14/15)

Answers for page 14

• The artist probably concentrated on the changing arms because leafy branches are eye-catching and make the picture look more dramatic.
• Apollo feels adoration for Daphne. She sneers, as if mocking him.
• Apollo's raised leg and flowing scarf show that he has been running.
• The river is a symbol of the river god, Daphne's father.

ABOUT ANTONIO DEL POLLAIUOLO

Antonio del Pollaiuolo (c1432-1498) and his brother Piero were important goldsmiths, sculptors and painters from Florence, Italy. They made works of art for their city and its cathedral, and for wealthy families. Antonio painted small mythological paintings in a delicate, jewel-like manner, often for chests or cupboards. He is also famous for making engravings.

Answers for page 15

• The carpet of flowers is a reminder that Narcissus will soon become a flower as well.
• The 13 birds include a peacock, a heron and a partridge. There are also three rabbits, a stoat and a long-tailed animal, like a fox.

ABOUT TRADITIONAL TAPESTRY MAKERS

Tapestries of this kind were traditionally made by a group of highly skilled weavers, who worked together on a loom. They followed a design drawn by an artist. Popular subjects were myths, battles, celebrations and Biblical scenes. The weavers used wool, silk and even gold and silver thread. Vegetable dyes were used to colour the wool. Over the centuries, yellows and greens have faded more than reds and blues, which is why old tapestries often have a purplish tinge.

FISHY FRIENDS (pages 18/19)

Answers for page 19

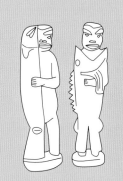

• The sculptures are the same height. The two human faces have similar hair, eyebrows, eyes and expressions. Both left arms are bent. Both sculptures have separated legs, joined to an oval stand. They are both painted in a mixture of red, blue and black.
• The fish are shown vertically, to echo the standing figures. The tails of both fish double as legs.
• The moon, a seal, a squid and a starfish are attached to the mermaid. These are all things that connect with the sea (the moon symbolises the tide).

ABOUT NATIVE AMERICAN CARVINGS

Carvers from the Northwest Pacific Coast of America were known for their wooden masks, rattles and statues, depicting mainly animals from their mythology. These included the raven, the frog and the 'bear mother'. They also carved tall totem poles that stood as family crests.

ABOUT JOSEFINA AGUILAR

Josefina Aguilar works in Oc otlan, the small Mexican village where she grew up. She uses local clay to model her pieces, which have a simple, playful style. The models are baked in a large open fire and then painted in bright, lively colours.

FLYING AND FALLING (pages 22/23)

Answers for page 22 and 23

• Icarus could be falling or soaring – it's impossible to tell for sure. The interpretation is up to the viewer.

• The red spot is Icarus' heart. It symbolises his feelings.
• Icarus lifts his arms, but his legs look heavy. His turned head could suggest excitement or shame.
• Chagall painted the sky around Icarus yellow and the ground below him red, to suggest the intense heat of the sun. A red-hot glow comes off Icarus as well.
• Some people cheer Icarus; others look dismayed and some ignore him altogether.

ABOUT HENRI MATISSE

Matisse (1869-1954) was born in northern France. He discovered painting while recovering from appendicitis, and then abandoned his law career to study art. He used mainly brilliant colours and patterns with simplified forms. In old age, too ill to paint, he made paper collages by sticking down arrangements of shapes cut from painted paper.

ABOUT MARC CHAGALL

Chagall (1887-1985) was born in Russia. He studied art in St Petersburg and then in Paris. As well as painting, he designed stage sets and illustrated books. During the Second World War, he fled to America. He later returned to France and created huge murals and tapestries.

DECORATIVE DRAGONS (pages 26/27)

ABOUT DRAGON ROBES

During the Qing dynasty in China (1644-1911), there was a strict dress code for the imperial family and their courtiers. The cut, colour and decoration of a robe indicated a person's importance. At special state ceremonies, such as New Year and weddings, they wore robes decorated with symbols from Chinese mythology. Only the emperor and empress (the highest-ranking people of all) could wear embroidered yellow silk robes like this, with five-toed dragons as decoration.

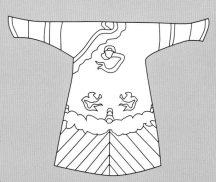

GLOSSARY

collage A picture made by sticking bits of paper, fabric, or other objects, on to a background.

imperial To do with an emperor or his family.

mural A picture painted to cover a wall.

myth A story about superhuman beings and imaginary creatures, often invented to explain natural wonders or local customs.

mythical or **mythological** To do with myths.

nymph A spirit of nature, pictured as a beautiful young woman.

pose The way someone sits, stands or gestures.

silhouette An image that is coloured with one solid, flat colour – usually black.

symbol A picture, or other kind of image, that stands for something else.

tapestry A decorative woven cloth, often used as a wall hanging.

texture How something feels to the touch.

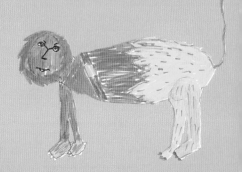